In Love with the All

IV

In Love with the All

IV

In Love with the All

Robb Thomson

To Nancy + Haynes

Enjoy

Robb

ISBN 978-0-578-96178-1
Published by Robb Thomson LLC
250 Alameda Apt 3310
Santa Fe, NM 87501
robbm@cybermesa.com

Interior design by Robb Thomson
Cover design by Eric Thomson
Font: Bembo

Special thanks to my daughter, Judy Thomson for her encouragement and insightful line by line editing. The writing group at El Castillo have been helpful critics, especially its former leader, Christopher Thomas, who has also edited the book. And I have been enormously encouraged by the editorial comments of Dorothy Alexander.

Thanks are also due to my son, Eric Thomson, for his design of the cover.

VIII

Contents

II
Brief Song

Coda

Introit

In a Hurry

My life hurried on today,
though I wanted to explore
the strange places along the way,
their teases and tastes
not to be found again.

At Even, I muse on the day
and find understandings totally missed,
beauties only glimpsed,
and bring closure
to a world that rushed
and would not slow.

I

HAIKU INSPIRED

LIFE

If it were without joy,
it would be laughable.

If without love,
hateful.

Without beauty,
pointless.

WE

feel in the singular
but live in the plural.

PROLOGUE

There are many paths
in old age,
but in every one
looms the question

what is it all about?

DAYBREAK

As dawn cracks,
spilling its yolk,
song erupts
to herald the burgeoning day.

Words Transcended

I know a sonata that suspends
all physical sense, and takes me
to where meanings
beyond my grasp
rule.

Silence

Beneath the silence linking words
lurks an undersound —
earthy and fecund;

though one word
is history for the next, it is only
from stillness the next chord speaks.

COMFORT

After a day of the bland,
utter simplicity —
just being.

DELIVERY

Bleak exhaustion stretches forever
and hints at death's grace —

when comes a gentle day
singing of being,

pure and clear.

SEARCH

We vainly seek
for final meaning
in all the distant places,

when it's won inside
beat by sounding heartbeat.

GROWING OLD

began in Kindergarten
when I graduated from
the slide to the handlebars,

and ended just here,
when I tripped over the edge
of my grave.

SONG

Knowing my heart's desires
like a river senses
oceanic rhythms,

my poem sings
the joy of being,
as it gurgles
into my arid days.

DAY TO DAY

How to live well
glitters untouchably
from the blue,

while in the muck below
we merely point a muddy finger
upward.

The Turn

Discord
spurred by garish day

is rendered a gentle mien
by the cooling hush
of evening's caress.

Nudity

The apple eaten to the core
and beyond to the seed
is the self
reduced to its purest —

kissing the skin
of the naked soul.

Bliss

From listless void,
love arises,
immaculate.

O Damn!

Here I am
reduced to the strength of a child
with a pill regimen that would choke a goat,
when I get the message
the other guests are leaving
and it is time to go.

Hell,
the fun has just begun.

KICK

The calendar says I'm old.
The doctors say I have problems.

But waking to the day
is still a big kick in the ass.

PINNACLES

Oh, legs that carried
me up the tallest peaks,

will you now carry
this world-shackled self
to the farthest heights of spirit?

The Parade

Days march like circus elephants —
trunk to tail,
parading through our lives
in ghostly strings.

But like no circus animal,
each has its own shape and color
to nourish our psyche with
newness.

Making Futures

In each moment,
I am unshaped, waiting
for the artificer within
to imagine patterns to be attached
to the twitching tails
of dangling memory.

A Poem

is words spewed
from a soul on fire,
forged in mindful will,
and trapped
in an opalescent cool.

Dwelling in Truth

What I would know surely,
I must know poetically.

No Hope

When I have charge of my fate,
like a squirrel expecting winter,
I hide nuggets of future
like puzzle pieces exactly fitted
to my dreams.

But when nightmares slash and burn
my psyche
I forget the hiding places
and become
a helpless wreck lost in perdition.

Hope

got left in a bottle,
and there it remains,
bobbing on an unending ocean
listening to the music
of our dreams.

Hope Out of the Bottle

Nietsche taught hope
only prolonged the torments of man
but Dickinson
talked about the thing of feathers
that perches in the soul.

We can prefer feathers,
yet when there is no relief
from defeats and weariness,
the song is very distant.

NEXT

I exult in the joy of becoming
as I sit in passive silence
and Mother Future flies through me
to become Grand Father past.

MEANINGS

take form from the shy feelings
that swarm near the surface
of Psyche, where,
diaphanous and elusive,
they seep into the sinews
to form the glowing beauty
of the artful human being.

THEM

People of simple beauty
who derive their joy
from merely being
illumine our shadowy seclusion.

THE HUMAN TIDE

turns and turns again,
leaving foundations
whose upper works have vanished,

ready for new people
and new beauties formed from
newly erected memories.

Horseshoe

The future is a bastard
with a horseshoe hidden
in his boxer's glove
ready to deal me a knockout blow —

when he can catch me.

Painless

With whispers of "it won't hurt,"
I felt the first backward lurch
decades ago
when bird calls receded into silence
and nausea clutched
at the retreating skirts of dreams.

There was no pain,
but how many more hints do I need?

LIVING WILL

In this now ancient body,
still
the breath is marvelous sweet
and each gulp yet fills it
with living will
as dramatically
as ever it did before.

PLUCK

We are fools
to grump over our fate,
when what we mainly need
is grit.

Evolution

is purposeless, they say,
but consciousness
— its finest work —
is haunted by meaning.

If that is not Purpose,
it is certainly
a giant unintended side effect.

Incandescence

Poorly sheltered in a body
dehydrated by the desert of life,
I hold, quivering in cupped hands,
the pure incandescence
of fragile naked self.

I am linked thus to the larger world of being —

flesh enlivening bones
of a starred universe.

To Live Well

is to learn to fail
without surrender
to ensure
there is a following round.

To Love Well

is to float quietly
in the river of being,

content to find
the ocean on my own.

Fellowship

is a summer shower pouring
from the hearts of friends
dissolving the bonds
of my tyrant self.

I and Thou

I can know more than one You
at once, but will the diluted love
I can manage be enough to bind us
if You are many?

To the New Year

You winked as we celebrated.

For those pompous resolutions
so gravely made
will have little to do with our futures —

the wink says it all!

Tamed

Like a mustang, free and wild,
is stunned into its taming,
our world, once fierce and vicious,
is reconciled to human ways.

Prayer

When I have learned to love
more perfectly,
When I have made
more perfect beauty,
When I know more deeply
the meaning of the stars,

then will I know
a more perfect being.

Being

To be is to experience
living as deeply
as possible,
knowing it to be
elusive as a fly.

Slow

is best,
for the small ones easily
skitter between the feet.

With limbs a-hurry,
I am stranger to myself
and amble a lonely track.

Spring Storm

The earth is carried away
particle by particle for safekeeping
in the caverns of the wind.

THE FLOWER

In the service of hope,
its beauty is possibility.

Fertilized,
an inconspicuous seed
commands the future

to be again
a flower.

BROTHERS AND SISTERS

We
are created brother and sister.
I sing when you sing,
hurt when you hurt,
and together we abide.

At Ease

The night is quiet —
only the unsteady beat
of my heart.

Day is far off —
I am content.

Let There be Love

let there be beauty,
for in the end
I must smile.

Amen

A final chord fades
into the twilight like a dying sun —
accompanyment to Nature's whispered
welcome home
for the curst and drooping wanderer.

Farewell

Dark the sun,
back into their holes the stars,
withered my love,
as one by one
you drop away.

Evening Song

In the waning dusk
my spirit floats
in the aether of shifting awareness
toward the shadowed gleam
of the gone sun
conferring peace.

Day's End

Though clocks continue
their rousing romp,

rest is an eternity
girt in a single heartbeat.

II

BRIEF SONG

Words

in my language bucket
have turned fickle and skittish.
No longer do they spring laughing
from its surface, but wriggle to the bottom,
where they avoid my searching hand
like so many eels.

When one squirms away,
I can trudge on, with
"Sorry, a senior moment,"
but when the debate hangs on
a single, precise word,
and I gag in mid-sentence,

what then?

ODE TO JOY

I turn aside from the day's
wariness and tedium
to caress the gift of life —
the sun-warmed
bud of my being.

I wish to waste
none of the prized
moments binding
the beats of my heart
on futile trivia.

There is, rather,
a joy to be cried,
a touch to be shared,
and the grand awe of it all
to dwell in.

Forgotten

In the dawn time,
to live was to be in union
with the Divine.

Now aged,
how do I learn to listen again
to first intuitions —

what have I forgotten?

A Long Night

With the stink of death constricting
my breath, I stare, but cannot see the glow
that used to appear in the East.
I fear the sun has lost its daily battle
with night, and may be on its way to hell.

In night's solid grip, I set up a shrine
in my cell to all those remembered daybreaks,
gestate new strength in the secret dark,
and plan subversive possibilities
for the unseen dawn.

DANCE

Alone in its night
my spirit knows
its meanly worth,
glances at death,
spurns her stench,

and begins a dance —

singing of love
to the beat
of a quickening heart.

Joy

Of all joys, the chief
is the surge of being alive,

of air going deep
into lungs,
the tingle of blood
filling fingers,
the oxygen of laughter expanding a room,
the cocoon of your love
offered in cupped hands —

the joys of a body
that lives for me.

THE PATH

The river path traces
a golden thread
of augury
through my psyche
on which I stroll
past darker selves.

LIVING

is the joy
of sunrise
delicately spraying
the clouds and mountains
with rampant color,
while you and I
softly touch
in our souls
with knowing.

Beauty in all its forms
suffuses us.
The universe round
confirms us.

We Have Yet to Learn

life is not a gift.

But a loan.

The rent is a steady offering
of our love planted like
the delicate beauty of an orchid

on the thirsting fields of life.

The Wind

whistling in the roof
speaks to my quiet in the tones
of a distant dove —

a language primitive
and seductive,

and in a reverie sublime,
immerses me
in the still joys of the celestial blue.

Making a Poem

Find words
to try the furthest limits of words,

find a music
to puncture thought.

and draw harmony
from the resonances of my heart
to free the joy in my soul.

The Will of the Poem

I clutch a wisp of thought,
or something seen
in an odd light,

think a poem
can be made of it
by following a subconscious
guide as it makes
its devious way
along the connections of mind,

and wander
into a place,
where a long sought self lives
hidden in a cave of the spirit
never lit before.

POEMS

must spring from the gut —
those that do
are gifts from gods.

Verse from the head
has to be born again
to thrive,

but many refuse
to endure such pain
and remain forever stuck
in uterine perdition.

My Quandary

Sometimes I am just me
and sometimes you and me at once.
At other times all your cousins too.

Nature is badly confused,
but never apologizes —
leaving me the hard work
of figuring out how I
can be all that together.

Fully Human

I am closest to being me
when I am caught up
in an ecstatic musical passage
or in tender contact
with the ones I love.

In those moments,
my engagement is total,
nothing else matters,
and I am encircled
in beauty.

PIXIE

Who is the delightful person
who just sat next to me
with her joyous nature sparking
the air around us?

How did she find her sunny self
in the infinite possibilities before her,
and fix it in her nature?
And how can I learn that heavenly
fixing from her?

DRIVING TO ALBUQUERQUE

I head south down the ramp into a landscape
welcoming me with massive arms
blued with distance.

As the scene evolves in slow motion,
the gods of the hills
do their stately dance
to a music
imprinted on me
along with early lullabies.

"And It Was Good"

is plastered over everything He made
though I ponder how a mere chunk of dirt
can be good or bad.

On the other hand,
if we're the authors
of the future —
the perpetrators
of any purpose there is to be —

maybe there'd better be
a lot of good in it.

Inventing a World

From behind the wall of my skin,
I behold the teeming life in the world beyond,

where, safe in myself,
I imitate that world
with a private puppet show
animated with stories
structured on
the human invention of love,

and a wistful hope that it
actually has a counterpart out there.

Ending Histories

We have seen many:
Savanorola ending Renaissance,
the mullahs destroying the Arab high,
Calligula gutting Roman civil life,
and we may be witnessing the great
American turning.

Some were indeed ends,
some only served to strengthen
a people's perseverance.

We don't know which
till the bell rings.

BEAUTY

like Jaweh, is a word
of so much weight,
it cannot be reduced
to a single symbol,
its direct use
a kind of sacrilege.

But, like that other word,
it lurks everywhere —
in the breath of spring,
every beloved cheek,
everything we elevate
to high meaning.
It is the root of all joy.

And we never fully hold
her silken curls
in our earthen hands.

THE FACE

The impossibly wrinkled face
chiseled into the bust
at the end of the gallery
snapped me into awe.

From the shock of its rugged beauty,
I descended into the peace
within the stone, where I sensed
that all can be brought together

when a life is a true whole,
and the one who lives it knows it.

THE GENTLE SELF

Awakening to
the caress of feeling,
the derma of my skin
opens like morning glories
to the rising sun,
and I wander into the best universe
I know —

a place of gentle and joyous peace
where all my awareness expands
into a dimensionless self-sufficiency,
infinite in all directions.

MAKING SELF

No one taught us how
to make ourselves.

A crowd of quarrelsome artists
before a single easel,
we dispute what the painting
is about or what colors to use,

till, rising from
endless failure and disgust,
beauty fitfully finds itself,

and the New
makes its relentless way.

Soft Hands

The first talk is of meditation
practices learned,
of how the self sinks
into itself under the breath
and how sweet it is.

How people
have found a new dimension
inside, and how their delight
has bloomed
with this new perfume.

But a second world lies
beside the first, when others,
like ghosts slip between breaths
to sit quietly beside
the silent Buddha-self,

and how the ambience shifts
as presence and soft hands move
back and forth from one to another
in the quiet.

Night's Shadow

When the rising sun chases dreams
into confused memory,
it shines through
night's shadows,
leaving them to hold on tightly
to friendly objects,
or hide under a leaf.

When the sun goes behind a cloud,
they peek out again
in joyous dance, but take care
to remember where they were.
For like mistletoe on a tree,
they embellish their linked day thing
and give it a beauty beyond itself.

This Morning

I looked for joy this morning,
but there was no cheer.
I looked for love,
but no one spoke.
Life was everywhere,
but I heard no song.

The sky was up, though,
and in its glowing blue,
joy became not merely a laugh,
nor love only a hug —

a song broke out
in the beat of my heart
even this morning.

The Lurch

Fury grows like stress
building on a geologic fault
till a rupture occurs, the plate shifts,
and over time a continent
alters shape.

Police kill a black man in Jefferson,
one in Brooklyn, another in Baltimore —
over time
a pattern of injustice clarifies,
and an entire piople
lurch to a new state.

THE BROKEN POT

As the Native American breaks
her pot when it has served its purpose,
so the human is told to acquiesce
when his tiny contribution
to evolution's march is made.

But what of my pot's
exquisite beauty — the best I can manage?
Must its living spirit be wasted
by an antiquated biology's
rule of Death?

You and I Emergent

I do not fancy a universe determined by its beginning
or one governed by chance,
nor even one governed by a God I can't grasp.

But I sing Alleluja!
for this unfeeling and clueless refugee
from the big bang
that has given birth in an immaculate conception
to the twin goddesses of beauty and self-awareness,
both nested in the human soul.

Carolyn

She is gone,
and we living encircle
her memory,
winding strands
of remembrance like
ribbons round a maypole,

and wrap our psyches
in her choice of colors
of joy and life
to cloak us from
the encircling void.

THE EDGE

Before the act
is a moment,
uncertain —
a time of edge.
The future yet unshaped.

It is a time that tingles and itches,
but it will not tell.

It is Now —
and only after the clock ticks,
will we know if history
goes uphill or down.

TOUCH

In reverie,
I revisit a presence
who sits, silent and Buddha-like,
at the center of my awareness
anchoring
my sense of being.

When my focus wanders,
your vision appears
with an electric jolt
as our touch opens each to the other,
linked through the living sky.

Beauty Flower Borne

Across the vastness between species,
the flower,
wrapped in its blue,
instructs me in the intimate
secrets of beauty —
a wisdom so deep and direct
that when I whisper of love,
my sighs are borne to you
on its petals.

Coda

By Touch and Feel

O soul,
I grip your shirt tail
as we wander the dark,
feeling our way
behind the flicker
of an uncertain flame,

though blest we are,
with a love uniting us
with all those others
who grope in the same
depths of being.

Oh yes,
it is dark in here,
but feel you not, soul,
the perfumed air of life
that thrills with
every gulped breath?

ABOUT THE AUTHOR

Robb Thomson grew up in El Paso, Texas during the mid 20's to early 40's of the last century. He was educated at the Universities of Chicago and Syracuse, and spent a career teaching and doing research in solid state and materials physics.

In retirement, he now lives in Santa Fe, NM and writes poetry. He has written nine earlier books of poems, *Arranging the Constellations*, published by Mercury Heartlink, and *Centering the Pieces*, *O Damn!*, *Wide Places in the Mind*, *Smiling Deep*, *Being* and *Possibility*, *Walk in Beauty*, *Things of Feathers*, and *Collected Poems*, published by Robb Thomson, LLC.

CPSIA information can be obtained
at www.ICGtesting.com
Printed in the USA
JSHW020835270222
23291JS00001B/12